Unbelievable Pictures and Facts About Eagles

By: Olivia Greenwood

Introduction

Eagles are very big birds of prey that have fascinated people for many years. Today we will be exploring the wonderful world of eagles.

On average what is the duration of time that it takes for an eagle egg to hatch?

On average it takes around 35 days in total for an eagle egg to hatch.

Are eagles able to swim?

Some eagles are able to swim while others are not, they are not excellent swimmers but they can swim.

Are there different names for male and female eagles?

It may be interesting for you to learn that both male and females eagles are called eagle.

What do you call a baby eagle?

Baby eagles can be called a couple of different things, they are usually called eaglets. Although they can also be called fledglings and hatchlings.

What is the correct name for a group of eagles?

We bet that you haven't heard of this word before, a group of eagles is known as a convocation.

Do people keep eagles as pets?

In most countries, it is considered to be highly illegal to keep an eagle as a pet.

Where do eagles usually build their nests?

If you want to know where to find an eagles nest you will need to look very high up on a tree, as they build their nests extremely high up on trees.

Do eagles migrate like other birds?

Eagles are very interesting birds as they don't migrate as other birds do. They can even stay in the same place for years on end and be okay with it.

Is it illegal to hunt eagles?

The truth is that in many countries around the world it is considered to be illegal to hunt eagles.

Do eagles keep the same mate for life?

You may be interested to learn that eagles actually have the same soulmate for their lives.

What do eagles symbolize?

Eagles symbolize many things, they represent freedom, success and even good luck.

Are eagles nocturnal or not?

Eagles are not nocturnal animals, they usually sleep during the night time and they are awake mostly during the day time.

Are eagles at the top of their food chain?

The answer is a big yes, eagles are known for being at the very top of their food chain.

Who are bigger female or male eagles?

Believe it or not, female eagles are larger in size than male eagles.

Do eagles have good or bad eyesight?

Eagles are known to have excellent eyesight, their eyesight helps them to catch their prey.

Are eagles solitary or social animals?

Eagles, in general, are not social animals, however, during their mating season, they become more social.

On average how many years does an eagle live for?

The lifespan of the eagle depends on the particular species of eagle. On average eagles generally live for around 14-20 years.

What type of food does an eagle eat?

Eagles eat all types of food, such as cats, foxes, deer, and even goats. They are carnivores and eat all sorts of animals in the sky and on the ground.

Where do eagles actually live?

Eagles can be found in many countries around the world. These countries include Egypt, Poland, Austria, and Germany.

How many different types of eagles are there?

There are over 60 amazing different eagle species that exist.

Manufactured by Amazon.ca
Bolton, ON

24766700R00026